COAST ROAD

Books by the Same Author

Creekwater Journal (1973)
Grass Script (1978)
The Skylight (1983)
Selected Poems 1963 – 1983
Selected Poems (1985, 1990)
Piano (1988)
Certain Things (1993)
Selected Poems (1994)
New and Selected Poems (1995)
Lineations (1996)
New Selected Poems (1998)
Lineations (1998)
Afterimages (2002)
Nameless Earth (2006)
The Land I Came Through Last (2008)
Cumulus: Collected Poems (2012)
Daylight Saving: A Selection of Poems (2013)

COAST ROAD

SELECTED POEMS

ROBERT GRAY

Black Inc.

Published by Black Inc.,
an imprint of Schwartz Publishing Pty Ltd
Level 1, 221 Drummond Street
Carlton VIC 3053, Australia
enquiries@blackincbooks.com
www.blackincbooks.com

9781863957021 (paperback)
9781922231949 (ebook)

A catalogue record for this
book is available from the
National Library of Australia

Cover artwork by Tom Carment
Morning, Scotts Head, gouache on paper, 18x25cm, 1979.
tomcarment.com
Author photograph by Warwick Clarke

TABLE OF CONTENTS

To the memory of
Dennis O'Driscoll
marvellous poet
1954–2012

Journey, the North Coast

Next thing, I wake-up in a swaying bunk
as if on board a clipper
clambering at sea,
and it's the train that booms and cracks,
it tears the wind apart.
The man's gone
who had the bunk below me. I swing out,
close his bed and rattle up the sash –
there's sunlight rotating
off the drab carpet. And the water sways
solidly in its silver bowl, so cold
it joins through my hand.
I see, where I'm bowed,
one of those bright crockery days
from so much I recall.
The train's shadow, like a bird's,
flees on the blue and silver paddocks,
over fences that look split from stone,
and banks of fern,
a red bank, full of roots,
over dark creeks, where logs are fallen,
and blackened tree trunks.
Down these slopes move,
as a nude descends a staircase,
slender white eucalypts;
and now the country bursts open on the sea –
across a calico beach unfurled,
strewn with flakes of light
that make the compartment whirl.
Shuttering shadows. I rise into the mirror
rested. I'll leave my hair
ruffled a bit, stow the book and wash-bag
and city clothes. Everything done, press down
the latches into the case

that for twelve months have been standing out
of a morning, above the wardrobe
in a furnished room.

Morning

Feeding chickens, pollard scattered like wet sand.

They jump down stolidly off their roost,
as an old sailor
with a wooden leg;
in there, underneath half a corrugated iron rainwater tank,
open-ended.

I'm stepping around the bare black ground,
wire-netting propped
on lopped poles.
Moss about, bits
of brick poking through, and bones.
Rusted wrench
pressed into the earth, jaws open –
an effigy of a lizard. Reeds.

In packing cases, one side gone, the eggs,
in dry grass.
On this cold morning, they're warm, smooth

surprising stone

almost weightless.
Bent over,
at the side of my face the silver
liquid paddocks, and steam.
My eyes and nose are damp, I see through my own smoke.

And I find
a calcific fruit, as if in the pockets of a vine.
Again
I pluck out some warmth of the wintry sun,
ovoid
in the hand.

What is beautiful,
said Ingres, is two colours, ashen or earthen, almost the same,
laid together.

Finding the eggs, the colours of dry sand –

I hold them up
as the boy David would have done
his pebbles from the brook,
taking my time,
to go out armed against the Philistine.

The Meatworks

Most of them worked around the slaughtering
out the back, where concrete gutters
crawled off
heavily, and the hot, fertilizer-thick,
sticky stench of blood
sent flies mad,
but I settled for one of the lowest-paid jobs, making mince,
the furthest end from those bellowing,
sloppy yards. Outside, the pigs' fear
made them mount one another
at the last minute. I stood all day
by a shaking metal box
that had a chute in, and a spout,
snatching steaks from a bin they kept refilling
pushing them through
arm-thick corkscrews, grinding around inside it, meat or not –
chomping, bloody mouth –
using a greasy stick
shaped into a penis.
When I grabbed it the first time
it slipped, slippery as soap, out of my hand,
in the machine
that gnawed it hysterically a few moments
louder and louder, then, shuddering, stopped;
fused every light in the shop.
Too soon to sack me –
it was the first thing I'd done.
For a while I had to lug gutted pigs
white as swedes
and with straight stick tails
to the ice rooms, hang them by the hooves
on hooks – their dripping
solidified like candle-wax – or pack a long intestine
with sausage meat.

We got meat to take home –
bags of blood;
red plastic with the fat showing through.
We'd wash, then
out on the blue metal
toward town; but after sticking your hands all day
in snail-sheened flesh,
you found, around the nails, there was still blood.
I usually didn't take the meat.
I'd walk home on
the shiny, white-bruising beach, in mauve light,
past the town.
The beach, and those startling, storm-cloud mountains, high
beyond the furthest fibro houses, I'd come
to be with. Caught, where the only work
was at this Works. My wife
walked, carrying her sandals in the sand and beach grass
to meet me. I'd scoop up shell-grit
and scrub my hands,
treading about
through the icy ledges of the surf
as she came along. We said that working with meat was like
burning the live bush
and fertilizing with rottenness,
for the frail green money.
There was a flaw to the analogy
you felt, but one
not looked at, then –
the way those pigs stuck there, clinging to each other.

To the Master, Dōgen Zenji

(1200–1253 AD)

Dōgen came in and sat on the wood platform;
all the people were gathered
like birds on the lake.

After years, home from China,
and he'd brought no scriptures; he showed them
empty hands.

This in Kyoto,
at someone-else's temple. He said, All that's important
is the ordinary things:

making a fire
to boil the bathwater, pounding rice, pulling weeds
and knocking dirt from their roots,

or pouring tea (those blown scarves,
a moment, more beautiful than the drapery
in paintings by a master).

"It is this world
of the *dharmas* (the momentary events)
that is the Diamond."

*

Dōgen received, they say, his first insight
from the old cook of some monastery
in China,

who was on the jetty
where they docked, who had come down
to buy mushrooms

among the rolled-up
straw sails, the fishnets, brocade litters,
and geese in baskets.

High sea-going junk,
shuffling and dipping
like an official.

He could see
an empty shoreline, the pine board of the beach,
the mountains

far off
and dusty. Standing about
with his new smooth skull.

The horses' lumpy hooves clumped on the planks,
they arched their necks
and dipped their heads like swans,

manes blown about
like white threads from off
the falling breakers;

holding up their hooves as though they were tender,
the sea grabbing at
the timber below.

And the two Buddhists in all the shuffle got to bow.
The old man told him, Up there,
that place –

the monastery a cliff-face
in one of the shadowy hills.
My study is cooking;

no, not devotion. No,
no, not your sacred books (meaning Buddhism). And Dōgen,
irate –

he must have thought
who is this old prick, so ignorant
of the Law?

and it must have shown.
Son, I regret
that you haven't caught on

to where it is one discovers
the Original Nature
of the mind and things.

*

"When you see mountains and rivers
you see the Buddha-nature. When you see the Buddha-nature
it is the cheeks of a donkey or the mouth of a horse."

And he said, Ideas
from reading, from people, from a personal bias,
toss them all out –

"discolourations."
You shall only discover by looking in
this momentary mind.

And said, "The world is in ceaseless transformation,
and to meditate
is just awareness, with no

clinging to,
no working on, the mind. Letting thoughts go
as they arise, we are borne on a 'marvellous emptiness.'"

As there's no abiding self
there is no delusion and no realisation,
no Buddha and no troubled beings.

Things tells us what we need to do.
Otherwise, we face the wall, cross-legged.
It is nothing but sitting. Not a grain of merit is obtained.

And upon this leaf one shall cross over
the stormy sea,
among the dragon-like waves.

North Coast Town

Out beside the highway, first thing in the morning,
nothing much in my pockets but sand
from the beach. A Shell station (with their 'Mens' locked),
a closed hamburger stand.

I washed at a tap down beside the changing sheds,
stepping about on mud. Through the wall
smell of the vandals' lavatory
and an automatic chill flushing in the urinal.

Eat a floury apple and stand about. At this kerb
sand crawls by, and palm fronds here
scrape dryly. Car after car now – it's like a boxer
warming up with the heavy bag, spitting air.

A car slows and I chase it. Two hoods
going shooting. Tattoos and greasy Fifties pompadour.
Rev in High Street, drop their first can.
Plastic pennants on the distilled morning, everywhere;

a dog trotting, and someone hoses down a pavement;
our image flaps in shop fronts; smoking on
past the pink 'Tropicana' motel (stucco with seashells);
the RSL, like a fancy-dress pharaoh; the 'Odeon',

a warehouse picture show. We pass
bulldozed acres; the place is becoming chrome,
tile-facing and plate glass, they're making California;
pass an Abo, not attempting to hitch, outside town.

Late Ferry

The wooden ferry is leaving now;
I stay to watch
from a balcony, as it goes up onto
the huge, dark harbour,

out beyond a gangling jetty;
the palm tree tops
make the sound of touches
of a brush on the snare drum

in the windy night. It goes beyond
street lights' fluorescence
over dark water, that ceaseless
activity, like chromosomes

uniting and dividing, and out beyond
the tomato stake patch
of the yachts, with their orange
lamps; leaving this tuberous

shaped bay, for the city,
above the plunge of night. Ahead,
neon redness trembles
down in the water, as if into ice, and

the longer white lights
feel nervously about in the blackness,
towards here, like hands
after the light switch.

The ferry is drawn along
polished marble, to be lost soon
amongst a blizzard of light
swarming below the Bridge,

a Busby Berkeley spectacular
with thousands in frenzied, far-off
choreography, in their silver lamé,
the Bridge like a giant prop.

This does seem in a movie theatre;
the boat is small as a moth
wandering through the projector's beam,
seeing it float beneath the city.

I'll lose sight of the ferry soon –
I can find it while it's on darkness,
like tasting honeycomb,
filled as it is with its yellow light.

Flames and Dangling Wire

On a highway over the marshland.
Off to one side, the smoke of different fires in a row,
like fingers spread and dragged to smudge:
it is a rubbish dump, always burning.

Behind us, the city
driven like stakes into the earth.
A waterbird lifts above this swamp
as a turtle moves on the Galapagos shore.

We turn off down a gravel road,
approaching the dump. All the air wobbles
in a cheap mirror.
There is fog over the hot sun.

Now the distant buildings are stencilled in the smoke.
And we come to a landscape of tin cans,
of cars like skulls,
that is rolling in its sand dune shapes.

Amongst these vast grey plastic sheets of heat,
shadowy figures
who seem engaged in identifying the dead –
they are the attendants, in overalls and goggles,

forking over rubbish on the dampened fires.
A sour smoke
is hauled out everywhere,
thin, like rope. And there are others moving – scavengers.

As in hell the devils
might poke about through our souls, after scraps
of appetite
with which to stimulate themselves,

so these figures
seem to be wandering, in despondence, with an eternity
where they can find
some peculiar sensation.

We get out and move about also.
The smell is huge,
blasting the mouth dry:
the tons of rotten newspaper, and great cuds of cloth . . .

And standing where I see the mirage of the city
I realise I am in the future.
This is how it shall be after men have gone.
It will be made of things that worked.

A labourer hoists an unidentifiable mulch
on his fork, throws it in the flame:
something flaps
like the rag held up in "The Raft of the Medusa."

We approach another, through the smoke,
and for a moment he seems that demon with the long barge pole.
 – It is a man, wiping his eyes.
Someone who worked here would have to weep,

and so we speak. The rims beneath his eyes are wet
as an oyster, and red.
Knowing all that he does about us,
how can he avoid a hatred of men?

Going on, I notice an old radio, that spills
its dangling wire –
and I realise that somewhere the voices it received
are still travelling,

skidding away, riddled, around the arc of the universe;
and with them, the horse-laughs, and the Chopin
which was the sound of the curtains lifting,
one time, to a coast of light.

The Dusk

A kangaroo is standing up, and dwindling like a plant
with a single bud.
Fur combed into a crest
along the inside length of its body,
a bow-wave
under slanted light, out in the harbour.

And its fine unlined face is held on the cool air;
a face in which you feel
the small thrust-forward teeth lying in the lower jaw,
grass-stained and sharp.
Standing beyond a wire fence, in weeds,
against the bush that is like a wandering smoke.

Mushroom-coloured,
and its white chest, the underside of a growing mushroom,
in the last daylight.

The tail is trailing heavily as a lizard lying concealed.

It turns its head like a mannequin
toward the fibro shack,
and holds the forepaws
as though offering to have them bound.

An old man pauses on a dirt path in his vegetable garden,
where a cabbage moth puppet-leaps and jiggles wildly
in the cooling sunbeams,
the bucket still swinging in his hand.

And the kangaroo settles down, pronged,
then lifts itself
carefully, like a package passed over from both arms –

The now curved-up tail is rocking gently counterweight behind
as it flits hunched
amongst the stumps and scrub, into the dusk.

"In the early hours . . ."

In the early hours, I come out to lean in the empty corridor of the train, as it's crashing and lurching through the night.

A liquefied dark scrub, and paddocks where silverish-grey mist is rising, slowly as a stirred moon dust.

The orange moon, like a basketball fumbled on waste ground, is bumping among the tops of a dark forest.

In the frosty, thick night a single farmhouse light floats wetly as a flare.

I have lain awake in such a bed, and it has seemed to me, also, it would be sufficient to be one of those carried within this wind-borne sound.

(And I remember the mail train: a fine chain of lights, as I stood in the paddocks of a wintry dusk. Its sound was that of wind through the swamp oaks.)

Diptych

1

My mother told me she had often stayed awake
in those years, and of a certain night
at a rented farm,
on the end of the dark leaf-mulch of a drive,
where she sat in the doorway with mosquito-smoke,
listening for my father, after the pubs had closed, knowing he
      would have to walk
"miles, in his state," or sleep in weeds by the road,
if no-one dropped him at our gate
(since long before this he had driven his own car off a mountain-side
and becoming legend had ridden
on the easily-felled banana palms
of a steep plantation, right to the foot and a kitchen door,
the car reared high, and slipping fast, on a vast
raft of sap-oozing fiber,
from which he'd climbed down, unharmed, his most soberly polite,
had doffed his hat
to the terrified
young woman with a child in arms, behind the gauze screen,
and never driven again).
This other night, my mother was reluctant to go out, poking with
      a stick
under the lantana, down every slope,
and leave us kids in the house asleep, a cough
trundled among us,
and fell asleep herself, clothed, on the unopened bed,
but leapt upright, sometime later, with the foulest taste – glimpsed
      at once
he was still not home – and rushed out, gagging,
to find that, asleep, she'd bitten off the tail

of a small lizard, dragged through her lips. That bitterness, I used
    to imagine;
she running onto the verandah to spit,
and standing there, spat dry, seeing across the silent, frosty bush
the distant lights of town had died.

And yet my mother never ceased from what philosophers invoke,
from extending "care,"
though she only read the *Women's Weekly*,
and although she could be "damned impossible" through a few
    meal-times, of course.
That care for things, I see, was her one real companion in those years.
It was as if there were two of her,
a harassed person, and a calm, who saw what needed to be done, and
stepped through her, again.
Her care you could watch reappear like the edge of tidal water
in salt flats, about everything.
It was this made her drive out the neighbor's bull from our garden
    with a broom,
when she saw it trample her seedlings –
back, step by step, she forced it, through the broken fence,
it bellowing and hooking either side sharply at her all the way, and I
six years old on the back steps calling
"Let it have a few old bloody flowers, Mum."
No. She locked the broom handle straight-armed across its nose
and was pushed right back herself
quickly across the yard. She
ducked behind some tomato stakes,
and beat with the handle, all over that deep hollowness of the muzzle,
poked with the straw at its eyes,
and had her way, drove it out bellowing;
and me, slapping into the steps, the rail, with an ironing cord,
or rushing down there, quelled also,
repelled to the bottom step, barracking. And all,

I saw, for those little flimsy leaves
she fell to at once, small as mouse prints, among the chopped-up
    loam.

    2

Whereas, my father only seemed to care that he would never
    appear a drunkard
while ever his shoes were clean.
A drunkard he defined as someone who had forgotten the
    mannerisms
of a gentleman. The gentleman, after all, is only known,
only exists, through manner. He himself had the most perfect
    manners,
of a kind. I can imagine no-one
more easily and coolly precise. With him,
manner had subsumed all of feeling. To brush and dent the hat
which one would raise, or to look about over each of us
and then unfold a napkin
to allow the meal, in that town where probably all of the men
sat to eat of a hot evening without a shirt,
was his dry passion. After all, he was a university man
(although ungraduated), something more rare then.
My father, I see, was hopelessly melancholic –
the position of those wary
small eyes, and thin lips, on the long-boned face
proclaimed the bitterness of every pleasure, except those of form.
He often drank alone
at the RSL club, and had been known to wear a carefully-
    considered tie
to get drunk in the sandhills, watching the sea.
When he was ill and was at home at night, I would look into his
    bedroom,

on the end of a gauzed verandah, from around the door and a little
    behind him,
and see his frighteningly high-domed skull under the lamp-light, as
    he read
in a curdle of cigarette smoke.
Light shone through wire mesh onto the packed hydrangea heads,
and on the great ragged mass of insects, like bees over a comb, that
    crawled tethered
and ignored right beside him. He seemed content, at these times,
as though he'd done all he could
to make a case against himself, and had been forced, objectively, to
    give up.
He liked his bland ulcer-patient food
and the heap of library books I brought. (My instructions always
    were:
"Nothing whingeing. Nothing by New York Jews, or by women,
other than Jane Austen, nothing
'spiritual' and from the Russian.")
And yet, the only time I heard him say that he'd enjoyed anything
was when he spoke of the bush, once. "Up in those hills,"
he advised me, pointing around, "when the sun is coming out of the
    sea, standing among
that lifting timber, you can feel at peace."
I was impressed. He asked me, another time, that when he died
I should take his ashes somewhere, and not put him with the
    locals, in the cemetery.
I went up to one of the places he had named
years earlier, at the time of day he had spoken of, when the half-
    risen sun
was as strongly-spiked as the one
on his Infantry badge,
and I scattered him there, utterly reduced at last, among the wet,
    breeze-woven grass.
For all his callousness to my mother, I had long accepted him,

who had shown me the best advice
and left me to myself. And I'd come by then to see that we all
    inhabit pathos.
Opening his plastic, brick-sized box, that morning,
my pocket-knife slid
sideways and pierced my hand – and so I dug with that one
into his ashes, which I found were like a mauvish-grey marble dust,
and felt I needn't think of anything more to say.

Before Dawn

The whole sky, above the wide horizon, is adrift with grazing stars. Then it seems that these are dangled water, and the freshness of the night is breathed from them. In the dim fields nothing stirs, except, beyond a broken line of trees, which are slightly darker stains, a car's light is sometimes travelling. It is quick and soundless, along the farther side of the valley, like a goddess who goes running there, while holding up a torch. Soon we will see that she has lit the bushfire of the day.

Harbour Dusk

She and I came wandering there through an empty park,
and we laid our hands on a stone parapet's
fading life. Before us, across the oily, aubergine dark
of the harbour, we could make out yachts –

beneath an overcast sky, that was mauve underlit,
against a far shore of dark, crumbling bush.
Part of the city, to our left, was fruit shop bright.
After the summer day, a huge, moist hush.

The yachts were far across their empty fields of water.
One, at times, was gently rested like a quill.
They seemed to whisper, slipping amongst each other,
always hovering, as though resolve were ill.

Away off, through the strung Bridge, a sky of mulberry
and orange chiffon. Mauve-grey, each cloven sail –
like nursing sisters, in a deep corridor: some melancholy;
or nuns, going to an evening confessional.

Byron Bay: Winter

Barely contained by the eyesight
the beach is one great arc.
There overlap behind it
blue ranges, each a tide-mark.

Beside me, swamp oaks' foliage
streams hatching by Cézanne.
Out on the heath, a guard's carriage
follows the vats of a train.

Beyond, cloudy afternoon swells,
the colour of claret stain.
The sunlit town's strewn like petals;
its lighthouse a tiny pawn.

I turn, when far off. The sun brings,
because it's perfect warmth,
the feeling that I wear great wings
while stepping along the earth.

Curriculum Vitae

1

Once, playing cricket, beneath a toast-dry hill,
I heard the bat crack, but watched a moment longer
a swallow, racing lightly, just above the ground. I was impressed by
    the way
the bird skimmed, fast as a cricket ball.
It was decided for me, within that instant,
where my interests lay.

2

I remember there were swallows that used to sew together
the bars of a cattle yard.
I would sit in morning sunlight
on the top rail, to feel its polished surface
beneath my hands,
a silvery, weathered log that had the sheen of thistle's flax.

3

A cow was in the stocks with the calm expression of a Quaker,
and my father stretched his fingers,
a pianist seated on a chopping block. He bent his forehead to an
    instrument
out of Heath Robinson –
a dangling bagpipes, big as a piano,
that was played by tugging on organ stops.
The cow began to loosen its milk: its teats were disgorged,
the size and colour of small carrots,
and milk was flourished in the bucket, two skewer-thin daggers
sharpened on each other underhand.

Then, as the bucket filled, there would be the sound of a tap running
into deep suds at the end of a bath.
Finally, the calf was let in,
and that was like a workman building a big lather between his hands.

The concrete in those bails was shattered, but lay together
as though a platform of river stones; and water ran there constantly
from a hose, breaking up and bearing off
the hot lava of cow-pats. That water was delicate and closely-branched
as a long weed fluttering on a breezy morning.

4

There were great dents of cloud-shadow in the blue-forested
        mountain;
and far off, over
the paddocks, through midday heat, the fluttering silk scarf
of a light purple range.
Our mountain was the kite, and those in the distance, its tail,
through all the heat-wavering days.
And many broken, dead trees had been left standing about,
like stone ruins: pillars that held out the remnants
of cloisters and fine stonework,
with rubble beneath them. But the air was so clear, so uncrowded
with any past –
arbitrary corridors, unpeopled, through the air.
Room for the mind to travel on and on.
I used to stop, often, to stand there, in that immense amphitheatre
of silence and light.

5

I remember watching our three or four geese let loose and rushing,
with their heads beating sideways like metronomes,
towards a dam where the mountain-top hung;
and when they entered the water, the mountain's image came apart
suddenly, the way a cabbage falls into coleslaw.
Everything was changed, as easily as that.

6

Since then, I have been, for instance, in Petticoat Lane – pushing by
through narrow, stacked alleys,
among the tons of rotting garbage for sale,
and have seen the really poor.
Those people seemed just dangling paper dolls, threaded onto
a genetic string –
the characters of poverty, starch, lack of sun,
and stunted, hopeless spirit everywhere. Their crossed eyes,
twisted faces, snaggle teeth,
drunkenness were Dickens still, in '70-something,
again in '82. – People in greasy rags, on crutches, weeding wet butts
from the gutters;
spiky-haired, furtive, foul-muttering.
The women were shaped like slapped-together piles of clay. They
        scrabbled
amongst junk, viciously,
yelling at each other, and oblivious . . .

What is such an evil, but the continuing effect
of capital's Stalinism?
Enclosure, as John Clare has said, lets not a thing remain.
And then, an hour later, in the West End I found

how much worse I thought the askance,
meringue-coloured, prissy-lipped upperclass face – so sleek
in its obliviousness.
People go rotten with culture, also.

7

Another time, in Washington, when my girlfriend had gone
to see someone,
and while I was sitting at an upstairs window, I watched the bald man
who lived next door, after he'd argued once more
with his wife, come out to stand alone
in their backyard – round as a pebble, in his singlet,
but nowhere near so hard.
He was standing with chin sunk
holding the garden hose – a narrowed stream
he felt around with
closely, like a blind man's cane.
It disturbed me to see him like that – but then, as I started to
    consider myself,
I saw that I was walking
in those silver paddocks, again,
which as a kid I'd known.

8

Or travelling alone in Europe once, and staying in a provincial city,
indolent and homesick of an afternoon,
I turned, as ever, to the museum.
In such a mood, however, the masterpiece will often no longer serve:
it seems too strenuous and too elevated;
it belongs in a world too far beyond one's own.

From experience, one has learned to follow at these times that
        arrow, *École française*
XIXe siècle. There, on an attic floor,
unnoticed by the attendant, a newspaper crumpled
over his boots, or along the deserted outer corridors,
beneath tall windows, in the light from which
many of them are cancelled,
hang one's faithful mediocrities – in sympathy with whom
one had thought to be borne through until dinnertime.
Armand Guillaumin, Léon Cogniet, Jules Dupré, Félix Ziem:
no artistic claims can be made for these. Their sluggish or
        bituminous pigment,
greasy sheen, and craquelure,
their failures, so complex and sad, have earned them
"an undisturbed repose."
And yet, even these harmless,
unassuming and forgotten, as I glanced among them, on this
        occasion,
were forgotten
by their one idle, arbitrary re-creator,
and the landscapes that came far more vividly before my eyes
were all memories.

9

Into my mind there has always come, when travelling,
images of the twisted Hawkesbury bush
crackling in the heat, and scattering its bark and twigs about,
white sunlight flicked
thickly on the frothy surges
and troughs of its greenery; and within those forests,
great pools of deep fern, afloat
beneath a sandstone rock-lip; and of the Platonic blueness

of the sky; and recollections of Coledale and Thirroul
on their clifftops, where sea-spray
blows among the pines and eucalypts; and, most of all, of those
    forests,
cool, light-flouncing, with white female limbs,
and the yeasted green pastures,
where my mind first opened, like a bubble distended from a glass-
    blower's tube,
and shone, reflecting
things as they are –
there, where I have felt, anxiously, I would find them a while longer,
after passing Kempsey, once more, on the mail train of an early
    morning.

Fire Sermon

The lissome bay is silvered slightly, in its supine lightness;
a stocking-textured water
takes the morning's cerise.

But soon, between the headlands, sea and sky are solid blues
that have closed, almost
seamlessly, like stone.

And yachts have come out to climb on the sea's face, slow
and wavering – the way
that cabbagemoths walk.

These foreshores are deeply tented in eucalyptus saplings
and tea-trees, leaned
on the engorged light.

Here cicadas' sizzling strapped toffee strings of sound,
filmy and flashing, fuse
into sheets, all around.

Now the rhythmical light-points shoal the water thickly
as the shift to shovelled
gravel in cicadas' song.

Simmered eucalyptus oil vaporously uncoils, accompanying
angophoras, the dancing
Indras of rosy stone.

Dilated summer. It seems you can see into the Flame, while
light-cells teem, cicadas thrum,
to its naked sensuous events.

On the far shore, house-faces are hung, white muslin among
bush humble as rubble
in the blue Empire.

I have left everything behind, for an endpaper shore; to lie
under membranous layers, as
lights vault, coagulate, rebound –

to see one ignite another, billowing, and genealogies decline;
to watch here day's ardour
that turns water into wine.

In Thin Air

for Dee

It's songs of you that they play
while I eat alone
the grease of one more café
in an overnight town;

but the arrangements are made,
the paperwork's done,
and the money has been paid,
so I'm going on.

I'll have to go much further
before turning home.
There's kindness of a stranger;
the best is long known.

Icicles, knobbly as candlewax
that's long on bottles
or hung from candlesticks,
along the hotel lintels,

where I say your name to ingots
in purple night; to steam
above a few houses; to overcoats,
women inside, blown home.

The snow is shapely as meringue,
thousands of miles to come –
I have done such things too long.
Tips of obelisks in foam,

as we came by, were cemeteries;
a river, grey-veined marble;
the mauve, stiff-frozen smoke of trees;
snow smothering every gable.

A corruption is waiting hidden,
Conrad somewhere said,
even for affection so freely given
as ours; much is paid.

I lie in the long midnight train.
Thickly, black pinions fly;
we howl through a forest like wolverine.
Dawn's weird chemical sky.

Most of the day, keeping on
through Canada, I forget
the book I am reading, well begun,
because of looking out –

to wet black trees, snow-sprayed
one side (as if arc-lamp
lit), all of them fraying, then frayed;
to lakes, cold fat on soup;

to a young woman, in the snow
and steam we'd driven,
standing at nightfall to see us go
at a forest stop, on her own.

Plain houses, of doors and windows;
calcified silos, stables.
Out here, occasional light shows,
early, and warm as waffles.

In the Rockies, one's enthusiastic:
sunsets built of stone.
I thought of that haiku, "A firefly, look!
Forgetting I was alone."

There was a waterfall at full stint,
frozen to its rock,
like quartz or a stroke of paint.
We've stopped again. Taking stock,

it seems that I've gone far enough
to be offered normal life,
as though flipping over a disc.
I'd never thought to ask.

My life, I imagined, must be a hymn
to the optic nerve.
Other senses, you have proven,
will have all they deserve.

A Testimony

Gloomy midnight in spring, rain sinking on the canes in the garden.
I wanted some ease to my confusion, and reached out through
  lamplight for a pen.

I am one of those who have watched their image in the hearth,
  where a fire
was tearing itself to pieces, with its nails and with its fists.

And when shall I lie again in a landscape that is bright like satin
with my Venus of the sweet grass, her breasts as plump as quail?

Shall we sing hymn three six six: "Art thou weary, art thou sad?" As
  though it matters,
for who are we? Blowing in the abyss, these crying-out shapes of smoke.

The one perfection of the world is lust: is grasping, scheming,
  longing. And entirely of nature,
we're continuous with whatever binds the faceless pebble, which
  more truculently persists.

Along the bladed mountains and in the deep ravines, flowers come
  forth unknown to men
and pass away unseen. When it is spring there, a thousand bloom.
  Why should this be, and for whom?

Existence must come of itself, and it goes on and on without a
  reason, just because it is.
In human consciousness, it produced an eye. It has arrived where it
  might understand. Perhaps it cannot bear this.

We have envied the crane, her clear bright wings outstretched in
  flight, that flees the dark stormcloud,
seeking a shelter, and to safe shelter, to all her shelter borne.

We have envied when we thought how in the morning light, gently
    outpoured as from a tin,
that awakens Asia's folds, some dusty marauder puts forth its claw
    and retakes the earth.

For us, all is whirled away and is vanishing, as though it were the
    sparks of a trampling flame.
A thing comes into existence if it coheres with other things, but
    this everlasting fire lives on fire, on all of itself.

The first philosophers were the best, as well as briefest. "Everything
    is metamorphosis, and nothing can remain."
How can men have dreamed they would impose their demands
    upon the nature of this world?

There is a substance to things, which is ungraspable, unbounded;
    divided and passed on, like a secret inheritance; always present,
    in what is always passing, but never found in itself – it both is
    and is not.
Thus matter is profound; is *potentia*. And all that now exists is like
    the surface of the waters.

Things as they are are what is mystical. Those who search deepest
    are returned to life,
to ferns in a jug on the window-sill, to a burned-off hillside in the
    dusk that is like an opal.

To a spirited horse, chrysanthemums, a pannikin that drips,
    creeping vines, a cut, the corners
of the mouth, a bedspread, willows, a lump, shadiness, the bowels,
    bright salad, and dust above distant fields.

We are given the surface again, but renewed with awe. And I
    remember what I have to say:
Do not believe those who have promised, in any of their ways, that
    something can be better than the Earth.

Although, I say this with grief for all of those beings who are like
    shuffling, lumpy birds within a basket,
where they have spent or will spend their lives, and my heart feels
    suddenly stunned.

Again, as in a lit cavern, the headland's crumbling silhouette, the
    wind's emery paper glitter,
the serrations of the bay, and the paddocks, dipping into the sea.

Now a blossom slips through the tall wet boughs that are speckled
    with flowers. Beneath them, and above the hillslope's other trees,
out on the ice-pale harbour, one of the yachts begins drifting away.

Again, the dog is dancing on the morning dew. This black dog that
    will drape itself like an odalisque
amid the jacaranda's mauve shadow, at noon; that can make us
    seem a sickness of the apes.

What is needed most is that we become modest. And the work of
    art that can return us to our senses.
Our only paradise is the ordinary: to be fed by what is really here.

Now the sea is dark and harsh as shale. The afternoon storm, a
    swamp growth; sluggish bubbles,
above the whiteness of lawn bowls, on the small town's freshly
    painted green.

Looking out, from a verandah in the forest edge, onto tin roofs,
    drive-ins, supermarkets, fishing boats,
the ocean slopping by the tea-shops, the coarse cheese-rind of the
    beach.

In the smoky skirts of a brilliant immensity, the headland is
    sleeping like a paw. There, pine trees are shaped as though ink
    blotted
in the folding of a page. From out of those diffusing hills, an empty
    wet highway's light swallow play.

That road falls to offices and banks, to three spires (with their
    wrongly-directed penitence).
Now the bunches of the tree-tops are rolling; a white sail has gone.
    Slant rain.

In the late afternoon, I read on the verandah, and then look at
    the clear dusk; a striped towel hangs across the rail, beside the
    banana palms.
A single wing on the tall sea is passing the continents of the moon.

Description of a Walk

In the shape of long sand-dunes, but apple green,
the pastures I'd crossed. A quiver of rain
hung above them. One currawong somewhere, warbling
happily as a hose within a drain.

The forest was cumulus on stilts, from afar;
everywhere inside it, leaf-splatterings and spar;
the leaves, paint clots, or a fringe of trickling.
Angry as a burned insect, a distant car.

The forest closed. I climbed among sandstone –
great gouts of lava, petrified as iron;
puffed like fungi, or with a broken iceberg's edge;
all of a rusty red or burnt orange tone.

About the plinths and mantels was an artful
pebble-scatter; on its pedestal, an eccentric bowl.
Rose-coloured sandstone syncopated salt.
Blown rain was being emptied by the bushel.

Uphill, warped arcades of bush, rack on rack;
reiterative as cuneiforms. Bacon redness of bark,
or smooth wet trunks of caterpillar green,
and some with a close dog's fur, greyish black.

Other colours: Brazil nut kernel, an unfired pot.
In the wet, tart as bush smoke, a sweet rot.
The air rain-threaded, as though with insect sounds.
My heart flapped like a lizard's, by the top.

Underneath a clay bank, an old grey gutter,
now sealed with smoked glass. A claw of water
flexed nearby, on rock ledges and over roots –
a wide-toothed, vibrating cane-rake's clatter.

Sprigged trees; a vista of Pre-Raphaelite shine:
beneath gentian hills, a billiard table green;
ploughed land, pumpernickel; the road, a fracture;
the shapes of coral in a dark tree-line.

Rain shaded to silence. Then cicadas' shekel
sound. – Emptied from a bucket, a pile of shell
poured with the numerous headlong pour of sand
onto other shells. A dry calcite rattle.

This merely the start – the warming of an engine.
Each opens a row of gills; if you find one
you see almost through the body. Their joined hum's
power, an electricity substation.

I walked on and on, in such vibrance. Wet light
gave the leaves' undersides a tinfoil glint.
Rag and bone bushland. White arms lifted, dangling
cloth. That chant. What it was all for I forgot.

The Life of a Chinese Poet

In his youth, as he recalled, the Great Causeway of the Heavens
and Earth trembled
and the stars were spilled like dust, at the overthrow of a dynasty.
It could seem that he was old from birth, who was always saying
goodbye.
During eighty years he wrote five thousand poems, in a rhyming
prose or as songs for the lute.
Otherwise, his life was uneventful, except for the always-
remembered love that he had for a certain courtesan.
His mother refused to let him marry this girl, who was called
Scented Jade,
and soon afterwards he was ordered as a minor clerk to the far
province of Fukien.
There he discovered, at times, the consolation of nature – its
vividness, and its unthinkable reality.
He writes of the wild mountains, that were as sharp and glittering
as dog's teeth,
and that could be seen from among the hanging flowers of the
white lanes.
The river there he also admired, which he says was like the great
dragon of Ch'i
that turned upon itself in all the twelve directions, while subduing
the five elements.
It was his dream from youth to take arms against the Golden Tartars,
but the northern frontiers had been made safe; there was no
fighting, but only an endless boredom there.
At fifty-four, he went home to his native village, having never
gained a preferment,
distressed by what he heard of the luxury and incontinence of the
court.
He dreamed in his work of the "vast smoke" of chariots, as they
raced upon the plains;
he described his travels to far outposts, by night on a river that was
held in the moon's white stare.

Though he styled himself the Hermit of the Mossy Grove, and said
that he was wild, irascible and drunken, it seems he longed for
the company of other poets.

He had married a local girl, when she was fifteen, and spent most
of his time quietly lost in his books.

Pondering both the Taoist and Ch'an Buddhist teachings, he grew
more and more enamored of nature,

and found his companionship in mountains, rivers, and trees.

In rainy weather he would put aside his studies and trudge to the
inn, to drink with the farming hands.

"Daily the town inn sells a thousand gallons of wine. The people
are happy; why should I alone be sad?"

He was utterly sincere in his love of beauty. The thing he has seen
appears on the white paper. There is a sense of overbrimming life.

A Chinese critic has said, "His poetry has the simplicity of daily
speech; in its simplicity there is depth, and in its poignance
there is tranquility."

When he was seventy-one, the Mongols arose once more, and
began to attack the Celestial Horde;

the armies of the Sung were continually defeated, and were even
driven out of Szechuan.

Again, he applied for enlistment, but amidst the turmoil in the
corridors at the provincial capital he was pushed aside and
ignored.

Giving up all hope that before he died he would see himself in
battle, he returned to his village in disgust.

His songs were now being sung by the muleteers in far mountain
passes, by girls bringing silk to be washed in the streams.

In the capital, they were exclaimed over at wine parties, and were
murmured beside the Imperial Lake.

He was revered, if rarely seen, in his village, but finally one morning
the word went around that he had fallen hopelessly ill.

Everything was made ready – the thin coffin, the two thick quilts,
and the payment for the monks;

the earth was thrown out of his grave onto the hillside, and
the incense was bought that would smoulder among the
graveposts there.
But then, the next day, he rose on his couch, and called for wine to
be brought him from the marketplace;
he had the blind rolled up on his view to the south, and he wrote
some impeccable verses, in the tonally-regular, seven-syllable
form.

The Shark

There are tons of the sea's loose flesh above, made to jostle
and shimmy,
an immense, shadow-tainted
clear jelly.

It shoulders and displaces itself
about itself, on the peaked and scooped plain,
harried like migrant reindeer,
lava-bright or wind torn.

The diver goes on steadily sinking, spread on shadow
as if to drown;
weighted, he feels ducked and
pole-pressured down;

only his breath seems to panic, and he turns to watch it pass,
wobbling and clinking upwards
into light:
a stairwell that the mind climbs and breaks like glass.

The long sunlight sways here
in columns, as though a bundle of lift cables.
With its withered Native American head
a turtle's

struggling up steeply
on stumpy wings – an ennui, bound in horn,
a broken beak.
Bevies of fish are making little mouths to squeak

like society girls, in their spotted or banded
wafting chiffon,
and with impenetrable dead eyes. The jelly fish,
a huge heap of frog spawn.

Something stares sideways
that has Caligula's profile, and the teeth of an offender
in chrome. As a spinning hoop
when it's coming to rest surrounds a

centre, touching all parts of the rim,
so in leathern skirt the rat-tailed
manta ray, flapping,
is hung in the grit it's flailed.

The shark comes drifting with silent engine
through water thick as smoke,
a space craft called on by a distant gravity,
out of the murk.

It can loosely swathe
a limber grey fuselage.
It moves with all the potential and ease of someone
turning out of a garage.

The long body wavers beautifully
and easily,
as a train at dusk
through the curves in the floor of a valley.

The gills, for all their deepness,
are each neat
as a Japanese slit;
the head's simply rounded-off and incorporate

like the nose of a surfboard – it is not the authority
for anything within;
the head, amid jungle light, seems less important
than its fin.

It has the senile, yellow, ill-wishing look
of a hillbilly grandma's
uncomprehending eyes, and what seems her mouth
in its Greek mask melancholy or tooth-stump uncouth – .

But a foolish guffaw
and that vacuousness is filled with doubled barbed wire
or, closer,
a wreath, each leaf a razor.

The mouth is a picket of backward serrations;
the skin, sliding ground glass.
The diver waits with his single fang poised, for the tonnage
of its flick-pass –

imagining the voluptuous greedy wriggle
of its packed dog's body
and himself clamped too overwhelmingly, too rigid,
for struggle.

This energy, this pure appetite, that's
prior to the mind, this
is the thriving pathology
which is life; here elegant, as though wriggled from a thesis.

The effort to overcome it, in art, love, religion,
remains that devious will.
Nothing can be done about such greed, except to observe it
in hopelessness, which makes us still.

24 Poems

In the rock pool, grass
moves with the water. Violin bows
adagio.

I get up. Bright moonlight.
The sea is a glass brimming
under the tap.

4 a.m.; the Milky Way
blowing high above the forest.
A truck changes down.

Mountainside dusk;
white flowers through the bush,
the milking-shed lights.

Drying her eyes,
outside on the hilltop street;
hiding in the wind.

A railway hotel
in the rain. Reading early
by soapy yellow light.

Hot night. In the yard,
tighten the tap. It keeps dripping.
The mosquitoes come.

A cathedral –
long tapers of rain light
candles on the twilit river.

Two magpies stepping
on the verandah. Ploughed hillside,
smoke, and cumulus.

I sit and watch
the way rain is falling,
its eyes closed.

After a quarrel
she makes love in the shower
to the limbs of water.

The crows go over
all day, back and forth, anxious
to lace night with night.

A hospital room;
in the curtains, a slight breeze.
Thoughts of living.

Bring my mother in
from the morning, she will vanish
in that light.

The shadowy sides
of everything, on the way down
to the white sea.

In the vase, flowers
from deep in the heath
open their eyes.

Moon, a spinnaker
on the bay of night, and stars
make a distant shore.

Thick sunset waters,
golden as whisky. In this light
the tree-roots will walk.

Late afternoon sun
in the back of the shed,
cornered and still.

In the dim room
a piano-lid propped. Urgent
sail, far from home.

Open the door on
the gunshot of the morning –
work all day wounded.

Into the room, a breeze,
the pure note
on the ocean's single string.

A pious sunset
at the boatshed. Crows with gulls
along the rail.

In the bus, white neck,
black hair. Light has paused
on its endless journey.

The Circus

An old and unregenerate world
is overnight unfurled
on the park – something from the fifties
and from the medieval centuries.
It has changed less than the Church,
and comes to smutch
a wealthy reserve, beside the yacht club and tennis court.
I'm walking late
when the circus appears, through our liberals' confusion.
Without flambeaux: its power generation
is on a truck. The spatulate shadows of the workmen in a foggy night
unload at the point, by arc-light.
A ring-in myself, I have to go
on the harbour's deserted esplanade,
to watch in the dark how their settlement's made.
Almost at once, I see someone throw
a hefty sodden grey tongue,
among other offal, onto the lawn – it is trailing its long
ribbons, as if a bouquet
that's been ordered by a Salome.
The caravans are drawn up with their backs to the harbour,
now after midnight, and hunger
makes the tiger shout
in the shadows, pacing out
four strides and then back – dreadful to watch
the rapid tension of this match,
so dripping and furious.
Someone comes staggering toward the animals, solicitous
with a sloppy tub
full of snake-tunneled hearts and of watery blood.
But the tiger's meal
is a goat – a crying, sideways thing, among men's legs, which they kill
with a hammer
and the one accelerated gesture.

I leave; but am back at dawn,
when the workers are already out, also unshaven.
At this hour, the faces
of the men are furtive and bitter places;
they've teeth missing, and they smoke and spit,
and are ravaged or overweight.
People in line with buckets at a tap
and the portable lavatories have been set up.
I'm surprised to see
a huddle of dwarfs. One comes straight across to me, truculently,
glares out of his squashed shape,
legs buckled, hair in a "flat top,"
makes an abrupt, intrusive gesture
with arm and finger,
and instructs me to piss off; then he strides
away, ignoring the duckboards.
His brow is pressed in a deep crease, beneath its curlicue,
and his wide-splayed legs
are worked like an African canoe,
where one digs
either side, heavily, to row.
Such curiosity of mine is tactless, I know.
A foetid smell
of soaked straw and dung hangs over it all.
I walk toward the morse code, jubilant water.
Here they have sat, wrapped up, backed into a corner,
one of their old men.
Life shows this kindness to some, in getting them ready for oblivion.
The harbour's the only stardust and spangles
around here, but hard to ignore the circus, as it steps from its tangles,
the tent rising like a gown. I cross to the elephants, having seen
two accidentally bump and begin a routine,
a soft shoe, in slow motion,
swaying weightlessly, as plants under the ocean.

Then each is once more inert,
as though dangled from a crane. They scuff with a padded foot
occasionally, and scatter chaff
in a throw-away gesture that is like a hollow laugh.
Every inch of them is dried and scored
as a fence-board
among sand dunes. They're clothed with tarpaulins,
and have the loose tendons
of an old man's throat. Now the skinny girls appear, whose skin
is neon white. One hangs a lurid washing, and they lean
on guy-ropes a moment in the sun
(a baby who's tripped in the mud is no-one's armful).
They're dressed for rehearsal
in fishnet tights, drawn high on their loins,
and are loose yet sinewed. Paltry as coins
it might seem, but they have the discipline of their artistry,
as well as the cliché
they share with us, of longing and hurt.
The big cats are driven out
of their cages, into the tent – the carts have been drawn up like a
    tail,
and the animals, goaded on, trail
through each of them, well apart, from door to open door, then
    down a wire tunnel,
crouching, as into a funnel,
to burst forth, surging upwards impressively.
The tiger's last, and it runs the cages' full length directly,
low-slung, swift as a train engine
when unencumbered, treading each piston.
It can move fast as a wasp does in attack.
One hears a whip or pistol crack
in there. The male lion, with big grassy head-dress and tapering,
    dried stem,
went with a heavy clearing of phlegm,

resentfully. An emblematic flower,
wilting. It is toothless, no doubt, but like Baudelaire's the rancor
of the sideways looks,
to remind us of its reputation for a swordstick, of its gloveful of hooks.
Leaving, I see the old man
is dozing on. Set for a lookout, this graduand
has nothing to reveal, except to make us hope we perform
as calmly, in the face of final harm.
I look back and there is an elephant
being hosed, that's lambent;
and I wait a few minutes, to see if it wears for a hat
the day's crisp earliest yacht.

Beach Shack

It's overgrown with vines, but I
push out the gritty, cracked window,
just arrived. A usual storm,
soon. Grass is ochre, even so.

A slant fence, where currawongs fall.
The east seems tar, paint-slapped thickly,
and a scalloped surf keeps passing
along the headland, radiantly.

At most times drab, now the other
white places on this slope throw back
a light that's granular, over-proof.
Broken pickets, then water's black,

on which the foam rises and soars
to land, ablaze in its spread flight.
About the yard amble warbling
those currawongs, in black and white.

Philip Hodgins

(1959–1995)

Your funeral recalled me to your poems;
I seemed to find your touch upon it all –
the trees nearby, austere, sinuous gums,
their leaves rags on barbed wire; the lustrous call
of furious magpies; clay instead of tombs;
and low weather, with dry weeds and thistle
that we came wandering over, scatteredly,
to the coffin, strung above its cavity.

The empty place the world is hung upon.
"No speeches, only verse," in your dicta.
I read one of the pieces you had chosen,
"Sailing to Byzantium." How bitter
the humour, the irony you implied. Then,
because there'd dried up here part of the delta
of the Murray, it seemed right that Les spoke –
spontaneously brilliant, a common bloke.

Hartley and Paul read briefly. That was all.
Backyards of wooden houses, fairly near.
Each of us dropped down that infinite hole
a flower. But first, had to stand and hear
ropes slowly creak, unwound from a steel rail –
a labour to breathe, stopping; heads bowed there.
At a mullock heap, along a gravel track,
out in Victoria, some gold put back.

You were tough-minded as a classic Roman;
vehement and pure, a believer in style;
stoic, yet glamorous like Wilfred Owen;
the exemplar of an Australian school –
going straight for the pay-dirt of emotion,
laconic, pragmatic, and sceptical.
"Live another thirty years!" If I do,
it'll seem a moment, then. I'll think of you.

After Heraclitus

Late to lie awake
in a borrowed house in the country
in a forest of rain,
hearing its fine
traffic or the deeply held tone
of cello strings
softly drawn.
One knows oneself at this hour:
the range is guilt
or obsession with loss or fearfulness or fear
for another. One lies
drenched in thought.
The human is excess
of consciousness. For me
it has been the hands and feet
caught below the gunwale
from the dark
and I trying to pull those figures up
out of the waters –
they become inert;
they are unable to come in.
And there are others; although with them
it is they and not I
want possession;
and they are limber. I have been
unlatching them,
not too unkindly, I would like to think,
but over and again. "You will make it
on your own," I say;
"it's overloaded here,
we'll sink." Having to push away
faces I've known
or have loved. Economies
are imposed upon the heart.

I take up a book
and wish the day would break.
Even the tight
bulrushes, under the boughs
along the creek,
will be soaked full by now,
sopping in the warp
of lightning. A shimmer
from the garden –
the rubber gloves drawn on.
Women are nature's victims,
and we're theirs, and they are ours.
What rockets, what shout,
what furies
of hurt, what adhesive fire.
And wrapping itself
about itself, the ancient rain
comes reeling through the paddocks.
How exaggerated
one's regrets
are in the crisis, the crossing point,
of night. At daybreak
I lie on the floor
of an entangled pond, looking up
through the murk
to where the web-foot
leaves are treading
the surface, in dimness. I understand
"it is death for the soul
to grow sodden."
I hear what could seem
a paper umbrella, being tapped upon
with a Japanese
sparsity and calm. The sun

is able to kindle
in such a soaking world again.
"The sleepers dream
in a world which is each their own,
but the daylight world
is ours in common."
One steps into the river
as a river. Within an hour
I walk in the garden, hung around
by mulberry, persimmon,
palms with low fronds,
and oleander. In their shade
stand, more scintillant
than Manhattan's night, from an airline
flight, all these grass-tall spires
of rain. The wattle
that's clothed in spindled
leaves is thickly starred
with a shaggy bright water
as though it were the Milky Way.
I try to picture
how the light takes everywhere it rides,
across the valleys, across the hills –
those uncounted cells
of water, which are seeds.
There's a fruit lit
in the lap of each leaf, at the tip
of every black stick.
The close fields
are as ripe as oil paint; the longueurs
of the pastures
still wrapped in smoke.
In a wind, higher up
on the ridge, the tree-line is deciduous

as a clarinet.
Steam rises in the forest gate.
How this light exceeds Corot's
unshakeable dew. We know
there's no pause
to the brute secateurs,
and yet we must think Hail.
"Hail, holy light,"
although it's not the offspring
of Heaven's son – it is the lightning
from the start of time,
and our blessedness,
even as it keeps the nature of flame.

In Departing Light

My mother all of ninety has to be tied up
on her wheelchair, but still she leans far out of it sideways;
she juts there brokenly,
able to cut
with the sight of her someone who is close. She is hung
like her hanging mouth
in the dignity
of her bleariness, and says that she is
perfectly all right. It's impossible to get her to complain
or to register anything
for longer than a moment. She has made Stephen Hawking look
    healthy.
It's as though
she is being sucked out of existence sideways through a porthole
and we've got hold of her feet.
She's very calm.
If you live long enough it isn't death you fear
but what life can still do. And she appears to know this
somewhere,
even if there's no hope she could speak of it.
Yet she is so remote you think of an immortal – a Tithonus
    withering
forever on the edge
of life,
although with never a moment's grievance. Taken out to air
my mother seems in a motorcycle race, she
the sidecar passenger
who keeps the machine on the road, trying to lie far over
beyond the wheel.
Seriously, concentrated, she gazes ahead
toward the line,
as we go creeping around and around, through the thick syrups
of a garden, behind the nursing home.

Her mouth is full of chaos.
My mother revolves her loose dentures like marbles ground upon
    each other,
or idly clatters them,
broken and chipped. Since they won't stay on her gums
she spits them free
with a sudden blurting cough, which seems to have stamped out of
    her
an ultimate breath.
Her teeth fly into her lap or onto the grass,
breaking the hawsers of spittle.
What we see in such age is for us the premature dissolution of a body
that slips off the bones
and back to protoplasm
before it can be decently hidden away.
And it's as though the synapses were almost all of them broken
between her brain cells
and now they waver about feebly on the draught of my voice
and connect
at random and wrongly
and she has become a surrealist poet.
"How is the sun
on your back?" I ask. "The sun
is mechanical," she tells me, matter of fact. Wait
a moment, I think, is she
becoming profound? From nowhere she says, "The lake gets dusty."
    There is no lake
here, or in her past. "You'll have to dust the lake."
It could be
that she is, but then she says, "The little boy in the star is food,"
or perhaps "The little boy is the star in food,"
and you think, More likely
this appeals to my kind of superstition – the sleepless, inspiring
    homunculus.

It is all a tangle and interpretation,
a hearing amiss,
all just the slipperiness
of her descent.
We sit and listen to the bird-song, which is like wandering lines
of wet paint –
it is like an abstract expressionist at work, his flourishes and
then
the touches
barely there,
and is going on all over the stretched sky.
If I read aloud skimmingly from the newspaper, she immediately
    falls asleep.
I stroke her face and she wakes
and looking at me intently she says something like, "That was
a nice stick." In our sitting about
she has also said, relevant of nothing, "The desert is a tongue."
"A red tongue?"
"That's right, it's a
it's a sort of
you know – it's a – it's a long
motor car."
When I told her I might be in Cambridge for a time, she told me,
    "Cambridge
is a very old seat of learning. Be sure – "
but it became too much –
"be sure
of the short Christmas flowers." I get dizzy,
nauseous,
when I try to think about what is happening inside her head. I
    keep her
out there for hours, propping her
straight, as
she dozes, and drifts into waking; away from the stench and

the screams of the ward. The worst
of all this, to me, is that despite such talk, now is the most peace
I've known her to have. She reminisces,
momentarily, thinking I am one of her long-dead
brothers. "Didn't we have some fun
on those horses, when we were kids?" she'll say, giving
her thigh a little slap. Alzheimer's
is nirvana, in her case. She never mentions
anything of what troubled her adult years – God, the evil passages
of the Bible, her own mother's
long, hard dying, my father. Nothing
at all of my father,
and nothing
of her obsession with religion, that he drove her to. She says the
    magpie's song,
that goes on and on, like an Irishman
wheedling to himself,
which I have turned her chair towards,
reminds her of
a cup. A broken cup. I think that the chaos in her mind
is bearable to her because it is revolving
so slowly – slowly
as dust motes in an empty room.
The soul? The soul has long been defeated, and is all but gone.
    She's only productive now
of bristles on the chin, of an odor
like old newspapers on a damp concrete floor, of garbled
    mutterings, of
some crackling memories, and of a warmth
(it was always there,
the marsupial devotion), of a warmth that is just in the eyes, these
    days, particularly
when I hold her and rock her for a while, as I lift her
back to bed – a folded

package, such as,
I have seen from photographs, was made of the Ice Man. She says,
"I like it
when you – when
when
you . . . "
I say to her, "My brown-eyed girl." Although she doesn't remember
the record, or me come home
that time, I sing it
to her: "Sha lala
la la lala . . . And
it's you, it's you" – she smiles up, into my face – "it's you, my
     brown-eyed girl."

My mother will get lost on the roads after death.
Too lonely a figure
to bear thinking of. As she did once,
one time at least, in the new department store
in our town; discovered
hesitant among the aisles; turning around and around, becoming
a still place.
Looking too kind
to reject outright
even a wrong direction. And she caught my eye, watching her,
and knew I'd laugh
and grinned. Or else, since many another spirit will be arriving over
     there, whatever
those are – and all of them clamorous
as seabirds, along the walls of death – she will be pushed aside
easily, again. There are hierarchies in Heaven, we remember; and
     we know
of its bungled schemes.
Even if "the last shall be first," as we have been told, she
could not be first. It would not be her.

But why become so fearful?
This is all
of your mother, in your arms. She who now, a moment after your
     game, has gone;
who is confused
and would like to ask
why she is hanging here. No – she will be safe. She will be safe
in the dry mouth
of this red earth, in the place
she has always been. She
who hasn't survived living, how can we dream that she will survive
     her death?

A Bowl of Pears

Swarthy as oilcloth and as paunched
as Sancho Panza
wearing a beret's little stalk
the pear

itself suggests the application of some rigor
the finest blade
from the knife drawer
here

to freshen it is one slice and then another
the north fall south fall
facets of glacier
the snow-clean juice with a slight crunch that is sweet

I find lintels and plinths of white marble
clean angled
where there slides
the perfume globule

a freshness
like the breeze that is felt upon
the opening
of day's fan

Enku
sculptor of pine stumps
revealed the ten thousand Buddhas with his attacks
the calligraphic axe

Rationalised shape shaped with vertical strokes
I have made of your jowled
buttocks
a squareness neatly pelvic

A Sunday of rain
and like a drain
a pipe that was agog and is now chock-a-block the limber thunder
rebounds and bounds

it comes pouring down
a funnel the wrong way around
broadcasts
its buffoon militance over the houses all afternoon

Undone
the laces of rain
dangle on the windows
now slicing iron

a butcher is sharpening
the light
of his favourite knife
its shimmers carving stripes into the garden

And I have carved the pear-shaped head
with eyes
close set
as pips that Picasso saw his poor

friend who had gone
to war
a cubist
snowman the fragrant and fatal Apollinaire

The Fishermen

There comes trudging back across the home paddocks of the bay,
pushing its way
waist-deep in the trembling seed-heads of the light,
a trawler, with nets aloft
and motor that thumps like an irrigation pump
on the monolithic cloud. That cloud is straining out the sunrise
of a Bible tract,
which shows a few lumps of islands and the one boat
in the blazing sand-box of the sea,
while close-up the edges of such a volatile grit
are being swept ashore.

It is all noticed by someone in pajama stripes
and venetian slats of light,
at one of the wide bungalows
above the wind-moulded scrub, by two early walkers going down a
    track
onto the dunes,
from where they will watch the baggy sea that is practicing its
ju-jitsu on the kelp.

Only the harsh approval of the gulls
that the fishermen are back, the small boat
swimming heavily with nose up,
after a night far out on the phosphorescent plain, in a seething
    culture
of hatching snake eggs, or from deep
in an icy slush
of moonlight, the sea corrosive-smelling
and raw like rust. Back from the cobra-flaring,
gliding and striking sea, goaded it would seem by their presence
    there,
who tear
up by the roots the nets and lobster traps;

from a sea sweaty with stars, or one black and flowing like crepe;
a sea that erupts
and falls on them so hugely that only the radio mast could have
    shown
in the foam, if they'd had one. The fishermen have been taught
by each other that if swept away
in such a sea, without a jacket, which they don't wear in their work,
to swim down and make an end of it,
since they will never get back.
They live inside a dream
out there; everything they know about is in shadow,
who sometimes see a liner,
further off, go drifting past them like a town
on the moon,
and who see the ocean vomit a black whale
as if that were its tongue.

But you have come back, the pair of you, to a morning world
of newspapers and washed cement,
to swollen, damp
milk cartons, and car fumes,
to a train that comes hobbling through the edge of town,
past wooden tenements, with sand hung
in their eyebrows,
and a sky like bacon.

One of you has a wife, and she is brusque, earth-bound, and
    unforgiving still.
She loves you, you can tell, by her sullen glances.
Her humid-smelling nightgown
and the smoky curlicues of hair about her ears, in the steaming light – .
"Don't empty those boots there!
What the hell's
the matter with that kid? Give him

to me. Why must you always have this bloody soup for your
    breakfast? Look,
I'm burning it again. Do something:
watch it. No,
that toast is for the children!"
Who can know how strange the land is for you,
the place where you come to sleep?
You have watched the single mass of the mountains worked loose
that goes down aslant into the Underworld,
and alone then in the bow have seen the bear paws
of the ocean idly claw at you.
You see now, half asleep, the children eating – the grain comes
    undone in their mouths,
and you don't speak, you watch your hands, you once slapped one
like a wave.
And then you wake,
and all is silent. You stagger, scratching
at your underwear. The little cells of the screendoor
in the afternoon sun
are sealed with dust. Those big lemons, breast-tipped,
are new on that young tree, out alone in the concrete yard. On the
    table
the shopping lies agape
like a mouth of grief – the tins of tomatoes, red molars; the foam
    of the bread.
You give up, quite soon, tinkering with the bath heater
and write on the back of a note
a note, with a pen that half works. You walk through the glare
like someone taking a sick day, to the pub,
and again join the idlers there
in swallowing fumes and shadows.
The school kids come out shrieking in the sun –
such animals, you see, as you have released from your body,
in the hope of a little comfort, a home. What a delusion

that was. Children were to keep a woman busy
until you returned. In the pub, you stagger before you can walk again
on the water.
It is time to go out
with this bastard, your old mate.
You look up at him, where he comes to get you – his face
might have been some woman's nightmare;
a breath of sour acids,
and never a tender intonation to his voice.
You take your mate's hand, that is hard as a damp stone,
reached to you on the floor,
in the gutter,
in the sea. Through his broken teeth he tells you
to hold on, you will be all right. He pulls you into the boat
or he'll come out himself.
It can never be said, but you think, Where
have you found a love like this? In the morning, you and he
    separate once more,
with a few curt words
at the jetty.
You turn, to walk inland, along the gravel, and give earth another
    chance.

Flying Foxes

In the night, the gorging begins
again, in the spring
night, in the branches
of the Moreton Bay figs,
that are fully-rigged
as windjammers, and make a flotilla
along the street.
And from the yard-arms
are strung clusters
of hanged sailors,
canvas-wrapped and tarred—
these are the bats, come
for the split fruit, and dangled,
overturned where they land.
It is the tobacco fibrils
in the fruit they seek,
and those berries, when gouged,
are spilled, through the squall
of the crowd, like
a patter of faeces
about the bitumen. This amid
the cloudy shine
of the saline
streetlamps. In the ripe nights
the bats fumble and waste
what they wrest—
there's a damp paste
upon the road,
which dries to matted
sawdust, soon after the day's
steam has reared; it is scraped
up by the shovel-load.
The bats are uncorked
like musty vapour, at dusk,

or there is loosed a fractured
skein of smoke, across
the embossed lights
of the city. The moon is lost,
to an underhanded
flicked long brush-load of paint.
You think of the uncouth ride
of the Khan and his horde,
their dragon-backed shape
grinding the moon
beneath its feet.
And of an American
anthem, the helicopters
that arrive with their *whomp whomp*
whomp. I'm woken
by the bats still carrying on
in the early hours,
by the outraged screech
and thrashing about
where they clamber heavily
as beetles do on each other's backs.
They extend
a prosthetic limb,
snarl, and knuckle-walk
like simians, step
each other under
or chest-beat, although
hampered with a cape. In sleep
I trample the bedsheet
off, and call out
'Take that!' (I am told),
punching the pillow in the heat.
I see the fanged shriek
and the drip

of their syringes;
those faces with the scowl
of a walnut kernel.
It is some other type of bat
I think of: these, in books,
where I look them up,
have a face you can imagine
if you recall how you'd whittle
finely at a pencil
and moisten the lead
with the tongue-tip—
a little face that belies its greed,
like that of an infant.
All partly autonomous things
trample others down,
even what is their own,
and the whole earth is ground
or smoulders
with pain. No comfort for us that
of a night I have seen
how the living pass
about the earth,
that is deep in the ashes
of the dead, and quickly, too,
vanish into dark,
like will-o'-the-wisps
thrown out of the sun.
At three o'clock I gather
our existence
has been a mistake. I would like
to turn my back on
its endless strife;
but when I look out
at the night

there is otherwise only
an extreme,
the chalk-white, chaste
and lacklustre moon.

Wintry Dusk, Bellingen

There's a cellophane dimness to the world.
Three white cockatoos are raucous over
the moon's ulcerous face, that's now revealed.
Across the paddocks is passed a shiver;
and down through deep grass the dark fence posts ride.
Pointing everywhere, the dead trees gesture,
as if they were in panic when they died.

Home Run

The first time that you see the ocean from the North Coast line
is a place I have passed
very often;
it is "the prized, the desired sight,"
unearned, uncaught, that "parts me leaf from leaf";
nowhere seems to me more beautiful,
except maybe
the country between Gloucester and Dungog:
these are the kingdom of God
on Earth, especially
in the late or early sun. You know that you'll arrive soon
at this place on the coast, the first ingress . . . although, I am wrong,
I'm remiss;
there is a glimpse of the sea
and of an estuary, before that; no matter . . . you know you will
    soon come to the place I mean
when you've left Nambucca
and on either side there is a forest of paperbarks
in a swamp or reed-bed,
birch-like
saplings, long and thin, that push up
tightly together, and are glimmering, in the softness of the
    preferred hour.
Although, they can seem, rather,
to descend, with their slight waverings; to be runnels
of watery gouache,
the cream
of dampened woodash,
on a charcoal-dim
background – long dribblings
from out of the amorphous, smoky, olive mass
of their foliage.
And lying among these trees, you will see, is a creek
with many tendrils, like a root,

84

appearing everywhere, through acres of long grass, a seemingly
    broken water,
coloured like the water
we washed our brushes in at school.
Here you often slow almost to a stop
and roll above the swamp;
a slow tread
on the levee, the rail-bed,
while to the right the creek suddenly becomes a small lake, from
    beneath your feet.
In fact, it's an estuary,
hidden around a corner from the ocean. Across that light-sealed water
is a red clay bank
steep as a hillslope, with cursory, white, long-stemmed ideograms,
    very finely done,
scattered over it, the boles and limbs
of twisted gums, and the clumps
of their foliage a pale blue mildew. So you pass
through the ghostly *Melaleucas*
with their strangely wadded, loose-leafed bark,
which looks sodden and plumped,
but is a worm-eaten, dry, clay-white parchment. (Though if you
    take off
an easy handful of it,
there is a mushroom-pink or a peach-toned
delicate tinge
to its inner side: it is beautifully silk-lined.) You pass over a trestle
slowly, and begin to rush
again, through a close bush, among its scratched graffiti and
    chipped paint,
before that's rent
like curtains billowing open; and there, dazzling as the shock
of lifted plumes – light-speckled, and with a high-pitched note, it
    might seem,

it's so bright –
is the ocean.
This, after all night on the frowsty train, feeling half-sozzled,
sealed-in, air-conditioned,
and tasting of aluminum. One sees it
"silent upon a peak in Darien."
But the train leaps on
curving through the bush, inland now, like a dog off the chain,
into the clean,
lean dairying country; among the cleared paddocks that stage
the eloquence
of their single great trees,
to a massed audience of new-growth forest, shadow-faced.
This bright, mown country is being transformed by light that
    steams above the forest,
as a piece of toast is with its butter.
The long ramps
of the burnished grass lead away, towards a far-off plateau, a jacket
    on a chair-back.
And there appears an empty road, which we shoulder up against
and jostle aside,
our only rival, and it hares off, free,
not to be bothered,
weaving fast, unfazed, unslackening. It is the dusty
appealing colour of rolled-out dough.
And the grass, close by,
is the colour of powdered malt, or in some places the sable
of a Burmese cat.
The braggart light is on stilts.
Now you pass into a forest again, of glass-deep
shadows, among glass
reflections – the gum tree saplings, in a myriad white long stripes.
These are a downpour
that is splashing up ferns. The forest has the many curved forms

of cluttering umbrellas
afloat. And now, more bright pastures, although barely any cattle in
    sight:
they can hide, the paddocks are so billowing and vast,
in the warmer hollows. And here again is the lapsing and picked-
    up thread
of fine
lit telephone line.
It is like the swallows that come along with us; their progress,
although it's the inverse
in shape, is as supple and swift
as that of a porpoise.
But still, the first time that you see the ocean
from the North Coast train
is the great tune
in this production.
Of all the colour, this is the colour to have seen. The sea
is blue as ink,
or as a dye, newly pulped,
from out of which a great billow of fabric has been lifted,
the slightly lighter sky.
The light cells seem to exchange their energy, where they are lying
    on the ocean in long
transverse peninsulas,
so rapidly
that each photon is no sooner spent than it's re-lit
at the end of its quantum flicker. The beach is white
as a tablet of bath soap. There is a knoll
or sand dune
in the middle of the scene
from the top of which the long grass streams, something
    inexpressibly felt.
The waves stoop
with the shoulders of sea eagles and the gull-white feathers burst.

And you notice how the wind-paths, beyond the breakers, surge out
    across the water,
sinuous and spreading, like the arms
of the open eucalypts.

At the Cove

Early morning and I hang footloose in the ocean, out beyond the breakers. My legs could be seaweed tendrils, inside water that's a green smoke.

The suburb, set steeply above the beach, is obscured, as if it were an audience across the footlights. Already, hot sun reaches along the sea, and gathers between those dark brick bungalows the broken pieces of last night's rain, as bright vapour.

On the tented sea is a brilliant frost. Among its thin, strewn brocades, the water's ultramarine, much darker than the sky, which is a cobalt blue and unadulterated by any cloud. In salty eyes, the light becomes dazzling geometries, as when a cinematic lens shoots into the sun.

The wobbly sea makes me feel I am treading in the safety net beneath a trapeze.

I watch the waves' low-slung, stealthy approach to the beach: suddenly, they are moving faster; grown upright, they swoop on the shore, as though whooping American Indians, although the ragged hair they trail is white. They strike with an axe or knife, and make in the water the trajectory marks seen in comic books. The people who tussle with them manage buoyantly to survive.

From here, beyond the gulls roosted on the unbroken waves, the cove appears not much wider than my arm-span. The water has the raw smell of wet rust. I pedal on a one-wheel cycle, cranking back and forth to keep my balance, and idly play a little smooth jazz on the drums.

Sometimes I am taken up in a suddenly bulbous sea. The warm vague presence of the sky lifts me on its palm, to examine carefully such a fragile object, and then sets me all the way down. There are other swimmers further along who are exalted and relinquished in their turn.

I can make out on the hillside, as if through smeared glass, a row of thick-boled, widely peeled-open palm trees, among tiled roofs, at what must be a small park. The entangled blue smoke of the council's mowing machine is being combed out on the light.

Cars are shuttled back and forth as readily as abacus beads along the kinked wire of the shoreline road. There are big blocks of flats, like bakelite wireless sets, on the cliff-tops, above the leaping-up white poodles of foam.

And now, as if while I were eating humid, salty rice, there had been coolly slipped into my mouth a sliver of crisp watermelon, I taste very distinctly for a moment the wet smell of new-mown grass that has come out to me on the air.

Tamarama Beach, Sydney

Among the Mountains of
Guangxi Province in Southern China

I had been wading for a long while in the sands of the world
and was buffeted by its fiery winds,
then I found myself carried on a bamboo raft (I am speaking
    literally now),
poled by a boatman down the Li River.

A guest in Beijing at the Academy of Arts,
brought to the countryside,
I'd wandered out alone. A sheen on the night and across the
    ranks of water,
and close mountains that joined moonlit earth and sky.

When I saw the landscape around Guilin city
and realised it was still as the painter Xi Dao had known it,
in the T'ang period, I felt suddenly exalted,
as though I were riding in the saddle of a cloud.

The mountains' outlines were crowded one behind another
and seemed a wild loosening of the brush,
a switchback scrubbing, rounded or angular,
until the last fibres of the ink had been used up, again and again.

Those narrow blue mountains make endless configurations.
They are by far the main crop the province bears.
Zhuang Zu said that a twisted tree is not useful
and so it can survive for a thousand years.

A lead star plunged behind the mountains
as if the galaxy were crumbling more quickly than them.
How to convey the strangeness of this region?
I thought of migrating whales that break together, almost upright,
    out of the sea.

That suggests their power, but not their stillness.
Some mountains reminded me of tall-hatted mushrooms,
some of veiled women, among a laden caravan, but all had a
    corroded edging of trees.
We drifted by a few other rafts and their lanterns.

At times I saw rhinoceros horns, or a blackened cathedral,
at times the beauty of a carnivore's jawbone.
One place was as dramatic as a vertical wind-sock.
There was a broken palace in a fog-bound wilderness.

The next day we traveled to the village of Xin Ping
and found there drabness and squalor, a terrible indifference and
    listlessness.
Worst of all, the poverty in people's faces,
the smallness of those lives. Everything was the colour of dust and
    of smoke.

How can they not be embittered, and millions with them?
They see the comfort of cities, each night, on the communal
    television,
just hours off, and behind a stone door.
Earth could not bear the waste, were they all to have a fraction of
    what they know.

We, who'd alighted there for a few days,
could love nature because of its indifference, and found our
    freedom in that.
To do so, one must be secure. The same types of mountains were at
    Xin Ping
but I saw in them the sadness of eternal things.

The Creek

The slow effervescence of wind-lifted rain
on knuckle and cheekbone
a sweet
occasional prickling
that is met while I walk above the creek, having come down a lane
and out to the back
of the long yards at the edge of town,
a fragile assault
in the steamy afternoon.

The red earth's compacted in the high creek bank
baked tight
and a rope swing is looped
among the trees rising from beneath here that incline
through the element
of ointment.
These tapering swamp oaks are each drawn overhead
like a splinter that's festered.
The grass on top of the bank leads back to the plank
palisades
above one of which there perches a folded and dove-breasted
blue smoke
nested in the triple-ply of summer air.

And the green fretwork of a *Monstera deliciosa* plant
against the palings
is Matissean
in this unstylish small town, in the sleeping quarters
of the hinterland –
it seems the one reminder of *luxe, calme et volupté*
when our inheritance
is an Irish Sunday.

Grey weather between the high-grown, thickly-gathered trees, the
    lean
sparse-leaved eucalyptus poles,
parsley-
shelved, but with frail
grey-green leaves, and down the slope the kettle-black
lower boles
among which the water's glimpsed – the secret creek in khaki that
    beats
like a vein at the throat
of someone
who's lying hidden.

Here from an open place I once saw a slick naked black snake
quick
switchback swimming
through all of its two meters
along the creek, encompassing
it in swathes – a wound-up and then let go, fast
mechanical progression
into the dark
entangled mud; the crab
legs akimbo
of the black mangroves at the water's low margin.

But today there is only the egret's ancient Egyptian
délicatesse, its foot
professed
in profile on the bevel
of sand-
tipped shore. With its mosquito-fine
placement
I see it again
accomplish

a step, towards the swirl
of rain or of a fish.

The egret is shapely and tapering as an amulet
or a slim gourd
it's compact
as though smoothed between the hands
the neck
is kinked and finely drawn-out, which suggests a loose
length of vine
sharply trimmed-off, and it is seemingly ineffectual,
pensive.
One can imagine
as its claim that to pick the excess
from small life
is an honourable
scheme. It steps out of the stillness and stands
still again
and blue
like backyard smoke,
among the aimless insects of the sunlit rain.

Valedictory

I have come to an age where youth itself seems a virtue,
as beauty is, or wit. Her face was spotted
and her eyes were scared. She has renewed for me the phrase
"of tender years." Tenderness flourished, when we spoke,
as it can on a tree that's been lopped away.
I went by train along the valley of the Elbe,
travelling like Janus with my mind on her. I am one who is disposed
to believe grace of the body is a state of the soul,
and have been misled before. I have also been persuaded it is
     immoral
to encourage those much younger than ourselves
to offer up the unripe fibres of their heart. So I wandered in
     Prague,
among the human plague; the bridge was in darkness
and the crowds were restless and dark. The last question she had
     asked of me
for her tape-recorder was, "What is the question
you ask yourself?" I said, too easily, "I have no questions,
if that means I imagine there can really be answers. I am not one of
     those
who believe that the world has gone astray."
She looked at me with anxiety and with pity,
and wanted to talk. Therefore, young woman, I am travelling away
     from you.
(Also, I was urged by the driver to hurry.)
Now, I have the trams of Prague, the cobblestones, the dolls' houses
in pastel tones, pressed as it were out of jointed cardboard. On the
     way,
we came around the elbow and down the long forearm
of the river, which was narrow there and clothed
in a crinkled white sleeve. High up, like storm clouds, were
     rock-faces,
and beneath these the terraces of pale blue pines,

their branches shredded, down-trailing, each abashed as a
    retriever's tail.
In the tight valley floor, mustard-coloured flowers trickled through
    the grasses,
while close to the carriage window, the dark, twisted columns
were midges that fed on sunlight.
And I was struck, it seemed, with guilt, by the slow tolling
of a double-headed paddle, from a canoe, as we came by.
In Berlin, I'd had to ask
a question, myself, of a young woman, seeking directions
in the Hauptbanhoff. I chose, as one is inclined to on such occasions,
the most pleasant-looking person there.
She was standing in profile, and when she turned,
had a blind eye that was entirely silver,
like foil. I looked into this with a start, and of course
she was embarrassed, and I was embarrassed. But she was kind.
She did not deny or skimp her knowledge; but rather, carefully
    enunciating,
explained to me twice the way I should go.
Later, in the Pergamon, I found myself arrived before the famous
    bust
of Nefertiti, with her vacant eye, never restored – a choice
that it seems perfects her perfection – the queen of the slender
    throat,
who feels, you believe, the breeze on board an imperial ship,
as she is being carried upon swift oars. Dear girl
in Berlin, I wanted to praise your beauty, until you were as proud
as a sunflower on a bright day,
as drums, as a figurehead, as a shield, and an anthem.
Rilke has warned the artist
not to make himself ridiculous, in his years of recognition,
in his later years, through the undignified pursuit of younger women,
as he saw Rodin had done; causing pain and confusion, casting aside
with insufficient loyalty or care.

So many marvellous beings, whom we will never meet,
unless there is another life, or other lives.
This is what Whitman wished to believe – that we go on and on
along an open road, barefooted through the stars,
greeting others, with a clasp of them to ourselves. Hard to bear,
that we are shown these people who are like visions,
and yet never anything comes of it but that.
Such riches, which produce such poverty.

Thinking of Harriet

Years back, come to Japan, my step-daughter,
in our fifth-floor apartment, made a bound
from off the matting, and as she landed
the entire building shook. Her eyes were round.

Joan Eardley in Catterline

The black-faced sheep
are tilted in the storm-light and they face the black-faced
North Sea
from the long decline

of their swollen
pastures. Over all of this, the same
inertia. The weeds and fence posts come down and hang
above the lane

and we pass beneath
a bank that oozes like a luminous, wrung-out kitchen cloth. The barn
opens on a corner
its tunnel

directly out of the gravel
curb. We slide
by in a car, swishing over mashed cow manure and sliding water.
Joan Eardley

came here,
following the reports
on the news, to a place with the worst of
weather, to a cove

that in itself is as rough as the jaws of a wrench.
The tight cottages
are fastened to each other and to the headlands
of tight grass; one row on either. Otherwise, there is a pub.

She brought her cancer,
stepped down
into the rattling edges of the bay, with an easel
of lead pipes, it must have been. The storms here

are an opened furnace door
of wind and snow. She stood in the sea,
the water ahead
higher than her painting board,

as we knew
from Aberdeen's quiet gallery. The sea fell like a weir,
corrugated in black and white; the sky was seasick, a greenish-grey;
    the grey sea
greasy as stone, and its foam

urinous yellow, from the churned-up
shallow floor. Or else,
there was the release, the transformation, of peach blossom
on thickly-packed black sticks. She broke open

the paint, wound it together, squalled her graffiti
along the water's façade, scoured
with blunt spines, adjusted everything under a clunky spanner,
    undid
at the slice of a trowel,

dug her fingernails in, engrossed. Her subject,
death's approach,
become subject
to her.

Or she turned inland, into the passages of the sun –
to that over-ripe
pecked fruit,
which at other times seemed a snivelling, dangled

mucous, and at times had the liquid redness
of an organ
squashed into a jar. The sun, among
the broken panes

of the sticks
and the long grassy skeins,
waning,
was also painted as her own,

with an urgency occluding distance and time. Bits of straw and
    rope,
grass seeds and bent nails, were caught up,
among paint
that she lived in like the mud. Joan Eardley in Catterline at home.

I think of someone great,
of Dōgen, in his death poem. "For fifty years I have hung
the sky with stars; and now I leap through. –
What shattering!"

Minima

The beautiful in nature
is that which symbolises for us
a desirable state of being.

Reality can't be something
projected by our minds, since mind
is unable to affect it.

Apollo rides on
the shoulders of Dionysus –
otherwise is repugnant.

To be absorbed
in something is to have gone beyond
concern with happiness.

Our compulsions and motives
are as abstruse to us
as they are to other people.

The sense of quiddity
is mysticism
for materialists.

I have faith
that there is no such personage
as God would be.

We've come to fear science
because it brings bad news.
It is our only friend.

What is the neutral ground
we stand upon
when making our free choice?

Darwin shows us marvellous things,
the development of life, and of the mind,
occur entirely by accident.
(Possibilities need not be fulfilled.)

People who don't like
one's ideas often seem to think
that refutes them.

The only apology
for existence is
that it's so various.

Even if random,
quantum fluctuations
are an imposition.

We "affirm life"
because we must, but not
with all our heart.

Good is the conclusion
that we draw from evil.

Those who devalue pleasure
for themselves are likely to undervalue
pain for others.

Moral pleasure is reassurance
about human beings.
It is this we find so moving
in a work of art.

The senses can mislead us,
it is true, when we rely on
only one of them.

What we love about nature
is its unresponsiveness –
it is precisely
that it does not "care or know."

The sensory pleasures of the world
aren't merely transitory,
as the other-worldly claim,
but are constantly
renewed and refreshed for us.

Unselfishness has often
a selfish motive –
accolade (not the least one's own).

We feel nature act in us, and think
we originated the impulse,
but all our identification
comes after the event.

Épater les bourgeois? Certainly,
but there is another complacency one mustn't
overlook: *Épater les avant-gardistes.*

The human is a frail weed
strung with rain
in which the universe dangles.
But without that awareness
nothing in nature
could be said to exist.

Sanssouci

Frederick the Great's
summer palace, a rococo-style
pavilion, with windows
that could make
a glass house,
is the yellow
of Hollandaise sauce
and has egg-white detail.

It arises, encrusted with sculptural
gestures, on a billow
at the edge of a great park. Below
the blazing gravel
of its forecourt there is laid out
what has been the project
of his heirs, also –

the gardens. These are loose,
English, pluralist,
and proliferate
among copse and alcove,
gathering mist
in any niche or hollow
toward dusk. They've
shaggy hedges and rank-
looking northern trees
by Cranach,
are not at all Platonist.

Frederick came here
if he wished to be alone,
with just a hundred servants,
and played the flute, in thigh boots,
before banks of candlelight,
or walked the grounds with Voltaire.

He gave shelter, from Catholic
and Protestant, to La Mettrie,
who had pointed out
man is a machine of meat
driven by appetite
(there was a comparison made also
with a plant) – i.e.,
we are subject
to cause and effect.
Frederick composed his eulogy.

The Prince liked homosexual jokes
and saw his wife once a year
at a state occasion.
His nephew was his heir.
He wrote an "Anti-Machiavel"
and had four horses shot
from under him in battle.
He was a hero to Napoleon.

Although a *philosophe*
he built an army
of those who had no say
and took them
into hand-to-hand slaughter,
to break upon his hip
the sway

of Austria-Hungary.
As Engels used to quip,
History fulfils her purposes –
her potential – by wading
over stacks of corpses.

The clear-eyed Greeks
were in Frederick's thoughts
at Sanssouci,
as seen by the statuary
he'd planted
at each of the circuses
along the main graveled courses
and in alcoves
off the mazed pathways.
(At major junctions, as well,
there are fountains, each a simple
pool, with its tall
water like an ostrich feather.)

The gods and heroes here
are shown
at what they've always done,
which is bestir
trouble. Life
as the Greeks knew
is mischief. To interfere
is the way of Nature.
Aphrodite, though
she turns her face away
and covers breast
and pubis, is inflammatory
just because
of that modesty.

Beside her are displayed,
along with wheelbarrow and spade,
the usual abductions, rapes
and punishments,
in radiant nudity.

In one arbor
Hercules crumbles the spine
of Antaeus, who is embraced
about the waist, and hung
off the ground, a leg thrown
back, a toe feebly
reaching, to plug in
to the Earth.
Cinch of his girth
by half, his swollen scream
soundless, the extruded tongue
like a spear thrust
from behind, out of his mouth.
Undermined, the whole building
is coming down.

For those sauntering
of a late afternoon, the trees
and shrubberies
make a backdrop
to this scene, and are laden
with leaves, as a window
with blown rain. You see,
drawn near, in the level
glare, the foliage
is like tongues,
and it is these that the sun
lays its wafer upon.

Classifying the Animals

There are those that in the distance seem a swarm of gnats
those that with their barking try to rally us in a campaign against
    the stars
those that torment their prey
those that follow both sides of an argument
those that have broken a precious vase
those that can only be painted with a one-haired brush
those whose tongues light candles on the fingers of our hands
those that curl their tails
those that refute the Argument from Design, such as bedbugs and
    liver fluke
stupid ones, who lie still for a while and then run
those whose being is clenched, as though a knot in a frozen rope
mosquitoes
crocodiles
those that are bored
the good-natured beetles
those such as frogs and snails that are Enlightened beings
humans, born unable to stand
those that are fit to be emblazoned on a flag
those that should exist – unicorns and mermaids
unacceptable ones, unless we can make a great rational effort
those that cause people to smile – ladybirds, etc.
those that stir in us an erotic feeling
those that are easily broken and yet their kind continues to exist
those that one would like to be – the centaur, the phoenix.

Lines 5 and 6 are adapted from Jorge Luis Borges

Ekphrasis

Manhunt Near My Home by Irvine Homer

for Tom Carment

The artist was a farm labourer
in what he called "jam tin country"
and himself a captive
when he painted the escapee.

Nineteen-fifty-nine, Emu Plains –
there met at a prison farm,
where they were held for car theft,
the young Simmonds and Newcombe,

who broke out. One was caught
in days. This picture reminds
of how at fourteen I admired
that "Houdini," Kevin Simmonds.

Each day for weeks, the largest
manhunt in our history,
and yet the wireless told us
that again he'd slipped away,

despite 500 police,
with submachine-guns and flares
and a helicopter, and despite
the 300 volunteers.

For all the legends, rebellion
is light in our inheritance.
What outraged the populace
was in fact a mischance –

Surprised, in making the escape,
one of them gave a smack
to a guard, with a baseball bat,
and caused his skull to crack.

Something they had often seen
in a Saturday picture show,
but the sort of weight to apply
was difficult to know.

There are, I realise now,
further victims in such a crime.
They made him "comfortable"
with a blanket – waste of time.

The police look to their own
and moved like a bushfire;
brought back Ray Kelly, inspector,
who'd wanted to retire;

his style, an axe's bite;
the professed killer of three men;
in trench coat, felt hat, iced
spectacles; temper worn thin.

So Newcombe was caught. Later,
they found what Simmonds would do
was break into cars and listen
to the police radio.

He flickered through ragged suburbs,
eluding the blades of torches,
dissolved in misty streetlight
(food sometimes on back porches).

After school, with my bike, I had
the newspaper delivery
for a country town, and each day
paused, to follow this story

in different papers. Then pedaled
at twilight about the town
on gravel streets and grass verges;
the rolled newspapers thrown

into the yards I pretended
were sticks of dynamite
that would scare off the bloodhounds
and put the police to flight.

A rebel with cause – the suburbs.
Ahead of the sixties, his hair
was like Elvis. I admired him
more than any pop star.

And here he is in this picture,
near Newcastle, New South Wales,
a hundred miles from Sydney,
in a culvert as light fails.

Along the base, a dirt road,
at a see-saw's tilt, and under
this is where he's hidden;
above, two policemen linger.

To the left, the road turns in,
around a black, cairn-shaped hill;
from the right, a forest headland;
between is a skewed triangle

of orange grass, with wind-break trees.
Across this clearing, minutely,
the police disperse, clothes-peg shapes;
or like ants, you'd have to say.

Then purple forest, in long pleats
of cold slag, laid transversely;
light on undulant edges of
elided gullies. Poignantly,

a thin straight line of powdered smoke's
leaving. Lawrence called reptilian
the ancient stillness of the bush.
A dog; a coughing policeman.

And higher still, dark promontories
and a bleached ocean appear,
out of the Northern Renaissance,
by Altdorfer or Patenier.

An electric sunset: plum blue
to one side, with stacked thunder;
a new world in the other half,
its rosy and golden moisture. –

Canyons and crests of coral, a lit
engorgement; the confluence
of labile traceries;
a strawberry deliquescence;

some honeyed Apocalypse;
magnolias' scalloped ivory;
the bruised limbs of seraphim;
an orchidean Arcady –

as if in divine armada
Deity called on us at home
wanting to anoint the Earth,
our estrangement overcome.

This to balance Simmonds, taken
in a swamp, at twenty-four;
now open-faced, brave, resourceful,
but he would race no more.

Vengefully they'd seal away
all that he might have been.
Laying hands on him for photos,
Ray Kelly, brought to the scene.

Is that sunset meant to show
a heaven he'll never win?
Not an angel with its trumpet
nor a scroll has been painted in.

Is it to show us "the lilies
. . . on the banks of Italy";
that there's no separation
between beauty and cruelty?

The painter, self-taught, bed-ridden;
the brushes tied to his wrists;
both legs had been amputated
because he'd spondylitis.

Simmonds was put into Grafton,
the worst-reputed prison;
I saw the law as blood-stained
that well knew what would happen –

I'd heard of the "Reception."
In a few years, hanged himself;
grown tired of being beaten,
the only way to get relief.

I often used to imagine
there'd been a chance for him,
that a generous woman beckoned
as in a Hitchcock film –

Like Psyche, at the prow of time
that figure comes to stand
within the window's bay, a wand
of candlelight in her hand.

Earthly Music

The deer rise breast-deep
from the smoke
of grass-seeds
beside the lake.

"Butter in the corners
of your bread,"
grandfather advised,
a house-painter by trade.

A woman sponges
her side, one arm resting on
a cloud.
The magpie's song.

She scoops up her dog
(ours is uncouth),
an armful of soap
off a bubble bath.

In the crisp night
of a country town, as I amble
about, someone says, "Have you had your medicine yet?
Dinner's on the table."

All the wet day, lights burn
at the house opposite,
and gulls stand
in puddles about the lawn.

An owl floats over,
a balloon, so quiet,
its breast puffed full
of moonlight.

All day, the windows' grey weather,
above the Sound,
and waters file by
through the turnstiles, all day.

A cyclist in the country night, in a light
mist. His light
disappears in hollows for a while,
and then he comes on, with sprocket clanking.

So poor, we boiled all
our eggs for the week together.
Mum scraped butter off its wrapping paper.
We hid the ketchup sandwiches when at school.

In a new suburb, in light rain,
at the road's verge treading its line
with the stateliness of a tightrope walker,
concentrating, the diesel roller.

An old man's laconics
about weather he'd known – how the winds had held
at a slant the bull's
testicles.

On the small-town barber shop floor
snippings of black hair;
they're
exploded ideograms. Futurism in Japan.

A waiting room, near midnight.
His lips are moving quietly,
who's either semi-literate
or reading poetry.

Wing Beat

In some last inventory, I'll have lost a season,
through the occlusion
of summer by another hemisphere.
Going there,
the winter will toll twice
across the year. The leaves of ice
are manuscript
shelved on the air, and sift
fine as paper-cuts along the wind. I will go
to crippled snow
that rolls through crossings in its wheelchair, before the headlights
of early nights.
How glorious summer is to them
who have caught just a glimpse of its billowing hem.
"Fifty springs are little room," an authority
in loss warns, but statistically
I can expect to own
ten summers, before the heights of blue close down.
Although I've gone
northwards, I will cross the lawn
at home – the trees and yard in bloom –
in the mirror in an empty room.

ACKNOWLEDGEMENTS

The poems in this book were selected by Paul Kane for an American edition of my work, *Daylight Saving* (2013). A similarly compact and up-to-date version seemed to be of interest in Australia, so the file of the US book was provided by its publisher, George Braziller, for which Black Inc. and I express our thanks.

I would like to acknowledge my earlier publisher, Michael Duffy, of Duffy & Snellgrove, for maintaining my work in print over many years. And, as before, my gratitude to the Literature Board of the Australia Council for its indispensable support.

CPSIA information can be obtained
at www.ICGtesting.com
Printed in the USA
LVHW012201111020
668544LV00016B/1600

9 781863 957021